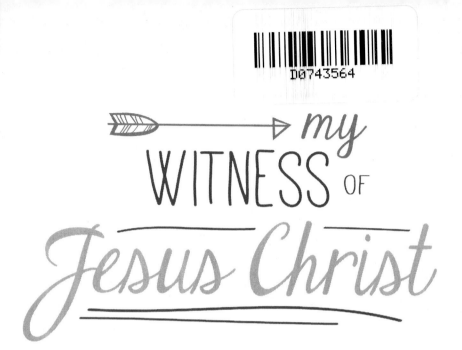

my
WITNESS OF
Jesus Christ

ISBN 13: 978-1-4621-1639-3

Published by CFI, an imprint of Cedar Fort, Inc.
2373 W. 700 S., Springville, UT 84663
Distributed by Cedar Fort, Inc., www.cedarfort.com

LIBRARY OF CONGRESS CATALOGING-IN-PUBLICATION DATA

Dorathy, Elizabeth, 1974- author.
My witness of Jesus Christ : Book of Mormon journal for youth / Elizabeth Dorathy.
    pages cm
Includes bibliographical references and index.
Encourages youth to read the Book of Mormon daily and keep a spiritual journal.
ISBN 978-1-4621-1639-3 (layflat binding : alk. paper)
1. Book of Mormon--Study and teaching. 2. Mormon youth--Conduct of life. 3. Mormon youth--Spiritual life. 4. Diaries--Authorship. I. Title.

BX8627.D65 2015
289.3'22--dc23

                    2015020777

Cover design by Shawnda T. Craig
Cover design © 2015 Lyle Mortimer
Edited and typeset by Jessica B. Ellingson

Printed in the United States of America

10 9 8 7 6 5 4 3 2 1

Printed on acid-free paper

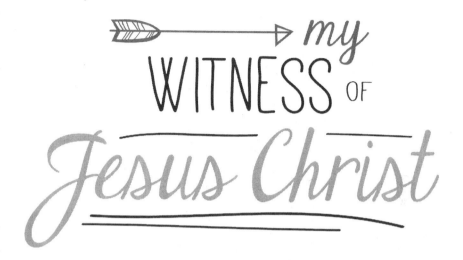

my WITNESS OF
Jesus Christ

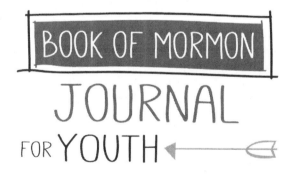

BOOK OF MORMON
JOURNAL
FOR YOUTH

ELIZABETH DORATHY

CFI
an imprint of Cedar Fort, Inc.
Springville, UT

Introduction

Taking the time to read scriptures each day will take some effort and planning, but it will greatly bless your life. As you read each day, you will feel the Spirit more strongly in your life and receive clearer daily guidance. President Ezra Taft Benson gave three reasons for why studying the Book of Mormon should be a lifelong pursuit: it is the keystone of our religion, it was written for our day, and it helps us draw nearer to God than any other book. He said, "There is a power in the book which will begin to flow into your lives the moment you begin a serious study of the book. You will find greater power to resist temptation. You will find the power to avoid deception. You will find the power to stay on the strait and narrow path" (Ezra Taft Benson, "The Book of Mormon-Keystone of Our Religion," *Ensign*, November 1986). This journal is to help you recognize inspiration from the Holy Ghost while you read the Book of Mormon and to help you relate the scriptures to your life. Start your study time each day with a prayer. After reading each chapter, answer the prompt or write any thoughts that came to you as you read. As you do this, you will discover answers to prayers, gain strength through trials, and come closer to your Savior and Heavenly Father.

Title Page, Introduction, Testimonies and Explanation

The last paragraph on the title page gives the purpose of the Book of Mormon. What do you think is the most important purpose of the Book of Mormon? How will reading it help you?

1 Nephi 1

In verse 13, Lehi sees the wickedness and destruction of Jerusalem and other catastrophic things, yet in verse 15, his soul rejoices and his heart is filled. Why? As you are surrounded by people making bad choices and negative things, how can you continue to rejoice and praise your Heavenly Father?

1 Nephi 2

What is the difference between Nephi and Laman and Lemuel? What does Nephi do to obtain a testimony? How do you relate to Nephi?

1 Nephi 3

When hard things are required of us, the Lord will help us succeed. What is one thing the Lord has helped you through or is now helping you through?

1 Nephi 4

Have you ever been "led by the Spirit, not knowing beforehand" what you should do (verse 6)? If so, write about it. If not, what do you think that would be like? What kind of preparation would you need to have that kind of experience?

1 Nephi 5

Thinking her children have died, Sariah has a trial of her faith. Compare her reaction to Lehi's reaction. What do you learn about faith from this story?

1 Nephi 6

What does Nephi say about what he writes? How does this affect how you will read the Book of Mormon?

_____

_____

_____

_____

_____

_____

_____

_____

_____

_____

_____

_____

1 Nephi 7

After Nephi's brothers treat him poorly, Nephi says he "did frankly forgive them all that they had done" (verse 21). Once Nephi forgives them, they are able to continue on their journey. Who do you need to forgive in your life so you can continue forward in your journey? What can you do to foster a habit of forgiveness in your life?

1 Nephi 8

In the dream Lehi has of the tree of life, notice the descriptions of the people and what they are feeling and doing. In verses 21-24, what words are used to describe those who are attempting to stay on the path and hold the rod? How do those words relate to your journey in trying to keep ahold of the rod? Where in this dream would you be if Lehi saw you? Where do you want to be?

1 Nephi 9

Nephi has faith to organize the plates how the Lord wants him to, even though he doesn't know why. He has faith the Lord knows more than he does. How does this relate to a specific situation in your life?

1 Nephi 10

After Nephi hears his father's words, he wants to know for himself. Why do you think Nephi wants to know and his brothers don't?

1 Nephi 11

Nephi wants to know the meaning of his father's dream. Why do you think the angel answers with visions and asks Nephi questions, instead of just giving simple statements of what various things in the dream mean? How do you think this example will help you when you have questions throughout your life?

1 Nephi 12

The angel shows Nephi the future of his people. What part do you think makes Nephi feel joy? Sadness? How else do you think Nephi feels as he sees these things?

1 Nephi 13

This chapter shows how people become confused about what to believe and stumble in their faith. What can you do in your life to gain understanding and remain strong in your faith?

1 Nephi 14

In verse 1, the angel talks about taking away "stumbling blocks." What is a stumbling block? Do you have any stumbling blocks in your life? What can you do to overcome them?

1 Nephi 15

Nephi feels that his "afflictions were great above all" (verse 5). Have you ever felt that way? How does Nephi overcome those feelings?

1 Nephi 16

Lehi is given the Liahona, which guides them. What in your life acts as a Liahona, guiding you and helping you find the right path to take?

1 Nephi 11

Laman and Lemuel see an angel and hear the Lord's voice, yet they are "past feeling" and cannot "feel his words" (verse 45). Why do you think that is? What can you do in your life so you can always feel the Holy Ghost communicate with you?

1 Nephi 18

In this part of their journey, a few family members are causing the entire group to have hardships and are impeding the journey. Sometimes other people's choices negatively affect us, and our choices can affect those around us. Write about an example of this in your life.

1 Nephi 19

What do you think it means to turn your heart aside (verses 13-15)?

1 Nephi 20

This chapter is a portion of Isaiah. Starting in verse 18, he uses nature to express symbolism. Which verse is your favorite? What does it mean to you?

1 Nephi 21

Who do you think the prisoners are that are spoken of in verse 9? What else could this verse mean? How do we make prisons for ourselves, and how can we help those who are in a spiritual prison?

1 Nephi 22

Verse 26 is talking about a time when Satan will be bound, but it also applies to our time now. What do you learn from this verse that will help you in your life?

2 Nephi 1

Lehi tries to help his children see all the blessings the Lord has given them. Write a list of the many blessings the Lord has given you.

2 Nephi 2

In verse 11, we learn that there must be opposition in all things. What does that mean to you, and how does it relate to your life right now?

2 Nephi 3

What thoughts come to your mind as you read this chapter?

2 Nephi 4

Nephi expresses a desire to be clean and never be tempted again. Have you ever felt like this? How do these verses make you feel?

2 Nephi 5

Nephi and those who want to follow God separate themselves from the others and begin to prosper. Why is it important that we surround ourselves with people who have the same standards and ideals we have?

2 Nephi 6

Knowing that the Book of Mormon was written for our day, why do you think there are so many writings about the house of Israel?

2 Nephi 7

What do you think verse 11 means? If you are creating your own light, whose light are you not using? How do you see this happening around you?

2 Nephi 8

What thoughts come to you as you read verses 24-25?

2 Nephi 9

This chapter is a great lesson about Christ's Atonement. Write down any questions, thoughts, or new concepts that come to you about the Atonement as you read this chapter.

2 Nephi 10

Verse 23 says we should be joyful we get to choose our own path. Why do you think agency is so important?

2 Nephi 11

Nephi makes a list of things his soul "delighteth" in. What are they? Does your soul delight in the same things? What do you feel deeply in your soul?

2 Nephi 12

This chapter starts by talking about the temple. If you have been to the temple, write about an experience you had there. If you haven't, write about what you can do to prepare to go to the temple.

2 Nephi 13

What do you think verses 16-26 mean?

2 Nephi 14

What do you think about this chapter? If you don't understand it, use the footnotes and read cross-references to see if you can understand it better.

2 Nephi 15

The Lord compares His people to a vineyard that isn't producing good fruit. What kind of "fruit" have you been producing lately? How do your choices affect your life?

2 Nephi 16

Isaiah sees the Lord, who asks for a volunteer. Isaiah accepts. Has the Lord ever asked you to do something for Him?

2 Nephi 11

This chapter is a prophecy given through Isaiah. In verse 14, he prophesies the birth of the Savior. Why has Nephi included this prophecy in his record?

2 Nephi 18

This chapter is about the importance of seeking the correct sources for knowledge, inspiration, and support. What are the best sources to seek answers to the questions you may have?

2 Nephi 19

What is your favorite title or name used for Jesus? Why?

_____

_____

_____

_____

_____

_____

_____

_____

_____

_____

_____

_____

2 Nephi 20

This chapter is about how the wicked will be destroyed. But it also mentions there is hope and some people will return to the Lord. What can you do to never give up on yourself or someone you know who is struggling with sin?

2 Nephi 21

Verse 3 says that Christ does not judge us with His eyes or ears. He judges us for who we truly are in our hearts. Who do you want to become? What can you do to change who you are in your heart for the better and become more like Christ? Make a specific goal.

2 Nephi 22

Isaiah says that Christ is his strength. Who do you rely on for strength? How can you become more dependent upon Christ for strength?

2 Nephi 23

Read verse 15. What is pride? Why is it so
destructive?

2 Nephi 24

Satan's pride is what caused him to fall. What can you do to stay humble and not allow pride to creep into your life?

2 Nephi 25

Nephi explains why he wrote the words of Isaiah. What have you learned from these chapters that relates the most to you?

2 Nephi 26

According to verse 29, what are priestcrafts? Do you ever do what is right for the praise of others? This can be a challenge for some people. How can you strive to serve and do what is right only for God, not because you want other people to notice how righteous you are? Why do you think it is important?

2 Nephi 27

This chapter focuses on the coming forth of the Book of Mormon. How do you feel about the Book of Mormon?

2 Nephi 28

Can you relate to verses 7-9? Have you heard these kinds of justifications? What is the truth? Why does Heavenly Father want us to make right choices even though we know we can repent when we choose poorly?

2 Nephi 29

Why is it important to have more than one book of scripture?

2 Nephi 30

Sometimes we compare ourselves to others, both inside and outside Church, and feel we are more righteous or better than they are. Have you ever felt this way? Why is this a dangerous way of thinking? How can you change this kind of thinking?

2 Nephi 31

What does verse 20 mean to you, and how does it relate to you right now in your life?

_____

_____

_____

_____

_____

_____

_____

_____

_____

_____

_____

_____

2 Nephi 32

What is the difference between reading the scriptures and feasting on the words of Christ? What can you do to make your scripture study more of a feast?

2 Nephi 33

Do you believe in Christ? How does believing in Christ change your life?

_____

_____

_____

_____

_____

_____

_____

_____

_____

_____

_____

_____

Jacob 1

What do you think it means to magnify your office unto the Lord (verse 19)? How can you do that?

Jacob 2

What did you learn from this chapter about wealth, pride, and priorities?

_____

_____

_____

_____

_____

_____

_____

_____

_____

_____

_____

_____

Jacob 3

What does it mean to be pure in heart? How do you become pure in heart? What blessings do the pure in heart receive?

Jacob 4

What do you learn from verses 6-7?

_____

_____

_____

_____

_____

_____

_____

_____

_____

_____

_____

_____

Jacob 5

This chapter is the allegory of the olive tree, which represents the house of Israel, or God's chosen people. How does this parable relate to you? What have you learned from it?

Jacob 6

What do you think it means to "cleave unto God as he cleaveth unto you" (verse 5)?

Jacob 7

In verse 5, Jacob says, "I could not be shaken." How do you think Jacob got to a place where his testimony was unshakable? How is your testimony? What can you do to strengthen it?

Enos 1

Enos prays all day and into the night. Take a quick assessment of your prayers. Are they fleeting and repetitive or soulful and yearning? Do you really feel like you are communicating with your Heavenly Father? How can you make your prayers more meaningful? Write a specific goal.

Jarom 1

Jarom says that the people stay faithful because they "prick their hearts with the word, continually stirring them up unto repentance" (verse 12). What does that mean to you?

Omni 1

Who are the different groups of people talked about in this chapter?

Words of Mormon 1

This is an insertion made by Mormon, who is compiling all the records several hundred years later. He is like a narrator, adding important information. What information do you think the Lord wanted Mormon to give us in the chapter?

Mosiah 1

King Benjamin gives his testimony of the scriptures. What touches you the most about this testimony?

Mosiah 2

How can you turn your "tent with the door thereof towards the temple" (verse 6)?

Mosiah 3

What does verse 19 mean to you? How can you put off your natural man?

_____

_____

_____

_____

_____

_____

_____

_____

_____

_____

_____

_____

Mosiah 4

What does King Benjamin mean when he says we are all beggars? When someone needs help, is it hard for you to not judge them? What do you learn from this chapter?

What does this chapter teach you about taking upon you the name of Christ?

Mosiah 6

What do you learn from verse 7?

Mosiah 7

Verse 33 gives us instructions on how to repent and be freed from struggles we may have. What steps should we take? If you are struggling with something in your life, how does this verse help you?

Mosiah 8

Ammon teaches the people the words of King Benjamin and then sends them home. When you return home after church, seminary, or another spiritual experience, what can you do to help unify and uplift your family?

Mosiah 9

Read the introduction to this chapter so you know which people this is a record of. King Laman gives an entire city to the people of Zeniff. Why?

Mosiah 10

What are the traditions the Lamanites teach each generation that causes them to hate the Nephites? Are there any learned "traditions" in your life that affect how you view or treat the people around you?

Mosiah 11

What does it mean to boast? Why is boasting a bad thing? How can you be more humble about your skills or talents?

Mosiah 12

Which of the Ten Commandments does Abinadi quote first to the priests of Noah? Why?

_____

_____

_____

_____

_____

_____

_____

_____

_____

_____

_____

_____

Mosiah 13

Abinadi quotes the rest of the Ten Commandments. Are there any of these you could live better? Make a specific goal.

Mosiah 14

Abinadi quotes Isaiah to introduce the idea of a Savior. Which verse touches you the most?

_____

_____

_____

_____

_____

_____

_____

_____

_____

_____

_____

_____

Mosiah 15

What did you learn from this chapter?

Mosiah 16

How does your knowledge of the Resurrection affect your life?

_____

_____

_____

_____

_____

_____

_____

_____

_____

_____

_____

_____

Mosiah 11

King Noah starts to get a conscience and almost releases Abinadi. What happens? Have you ever been in a situation where peer pressure made it difficult to make the right choice?

Mosiah 18

Verses 8-10 list the things we promise at baptism. Write them here and identify a few that you are doing well at.

Mosiah 19

King Noah tells the men to abandon their families to save their own lives. Are families today affected by the selfishness of one family member? What can you do to help strengthen your own family?

Mosiah 20

How does verse 11 make you feel about your family?

_____

_____

_____

_____

_____

_____

_____

_____

_____

_____

_____

_____

Mosiah 21

Now we are caught up to the point where Ammon and his brethren discover the people of Limhi (Mosiah 7). What helps the people of Limhi become humble and desire to change? What has helped you in your life to have a desire to become better?

Mosiah 22

What is the plan?

Mosiah 23

After traveling for eight days, what is the first thing the people do? Why is that important, and how can you apply it to your life?

Mosiah 24

When Alma's people cry to the Lord, what does He promise them? Do you think that is possible in your life?

Mosiah 25

Limhi and his people finally get to be baptized. How do you think they feel? How do you feel about the covenants you have made?

Mosiah 26

Alma is worried about those who are sinning. What is the Lord's answer?

Mosiah 27

Alma the Younger is described as a wicked man who is a great hindrance to the Church. What does Alma say about his experience in verse 29? Sometimes Satan wants us to remember our bad choices and not feel worthy or loved. How does the story of Alma the Younger give you hope?

Mosiah 28

What do the sons of Mosiah want to do after they repent?

Mosiah 29

Verse 12 says only God's judgments are just. What can you do to remove the judgments you place on yourself and others?

Alma 1

What part of this story relates to you and your life?

_____

_____

_____

_____

_____

_____

_____

_____

_____

_____

_____

Alma 2

The Nephites do two things to protect themselves: they arm themselves and they organize leaders. In your battle with Satan, what do you arm yourself with and who are the leaders you look to?

Alma 3

The Amlicites mark themselves so people know they are not believers. What sort of "marks," or outward signs, do you have that show people that you are a believer?

Alma 4

What sorts of problems start happening among the people?

Alma 5

Prayerfully consider the questions in verses 14-16 and write your answers and thoughts here.

Alma 6

Why do you think the Lord commands us to "gather [ourselves] together oft" (verse 6)?

Alma 1

Which verse means the most to you in this chapter?

Alma 8

Look at this story from the viewpoint of Alma and then the viewpoint of Amulek. What do you learn from this story?

Alma 9

Why do you think the Lord commands Alma to go back and preach to people who are so hard-hearted?

Alma 10

Verses 22-23 say the prayers of the righteous help those around them. Who can you pray for that needs your help? Who do you think prays for you?

Alma 11

What are your feelings and thoughts about the Resurrection?

_____

_____

_____

_____

_____

_____

_____

_____

_____

_____

_____

Alma 12

If this life is a time to prepare to meet God, what can you do now to be actively preparing?

Alma 14

Why do you think the Lord allows the believers to be burned?

Alma 15

In the conversion story of Alma the Younger, we see how someone who is struggling with sin can be turned into a champion for God's work. In the story of Zeezrom, we again see how someone can be turned into a great tool to help save not only themselves but many others. How can you relate these stories to yourself and the possibility of becoming more than who you are now?

Alma 16

What does it mean that they preached "without any respect of persons" (verse 14)?

Alma 11

What do the sons of Mosiah do that helps them "[wax] strong in the knowledge of the truth" (verse 2)?

Alma 18

Ammon provides an excellent example of how to do successful missionary work. What can you learn about missionary work from his story?

Alma 19

Why can Ammon not be slain?

Alma 20

The king's heart is softened because he sees the love Ammon has for Lamoni. How has showing your love for others affected your life or others' lives?

Alma 21

What does the word *zealous* mean? How can you become "zealous for keeping the commandments of God" (verse 23)?

Alma 22

Aaron goes to teach Lamoni's father, the king. How has he been prepared to receive the gospel? What experiences have you had with friends that may be a step to them someday accepting the gospel?

Alma 23

Thousands are converted because the king is converted and declares religious freedom. The king is converted because of the service and love Ammon showed Lamoni. How can the way you treat those around you affect missionary work?

Alma 24

In verses 7-10, the king lists blessings they received from God when they accepted the gospel. List them. Now list the blessings you have received because of the gospel.

Alma 25

The sons of Mosiah have been missionaries for many years and have suffered disappointments and hardships along the way, yet they rejoice because the Lord answers their prayers with success in preaching to the Lamanites. Why does Heavenly Father not always answer our prayers immediately and in a way easy for us?

Alma 26

This chapter is a great sermon by Ammon. What thoughts come to your mind while reading it? Mark the verses that stand out to you.

Alma 21

Read verse 8. How does the king's attitude here show the true spirit of repentance?

_____

_____

_____

_____

_____

_____

_____

_____

_____

_____

_____

_____

Alma 28

How can you find incomprehensible joy amidst your sufferings, sorrows, and afflictions?

Alma 29

What is the wish of Alma's heart? What is the greatest wish of your heart? How do your daily choices align with your wishes?

Alma 30

In verse 46, is Alma angry at Korihor for preaching against Christ and leading people astray? How can you develop compassion for those who may argue with you or mock you?

Alma 31

How do the Zoramites worship? What are some of the problems with this kind of worship?

Alma 32

Starting in verse 26, this chapter is considered one of the best sermons on faith. Write what you have learned about faith from these verses.

Alma 33

Do you pray throughout your day the way Zenos teaches? How does keeping a constant line open with your Heavenly Father help you?

Alma 34

What thoughts come to you while reading this chapter?

Alma 35

Why are the Zoramites angry that the people they had cast out went to live in Jershon? How does this story relate to you?

Alma 36

How can you relate to Alma?

_____

_____

_____

_____

_____

_____

_____

_____

_____

_____

_____

_____

Alma 31

Verse 6 says that "by small and simple things are great things brought to pass." Verses 33-46 tells of some small and simple things we can do in our lives. List some of these things.

Alma 38

What advice does Alma give to his son Shiblon?

Alma 39

Alma tells Corianton of Corianton's many sins. In verse 2, Alma says that pride is what started Corianton's problems. How does pride lead to sin?

Alma 40

Alma starts to teach his son the basics of the gospel. Why do you think he starts with repentance?

Alma 41

This chapter is about choices and consequences. Those who choose good receive happiness, and those who sin do not. However, this chapter is not complete without the next chapter. Write about what you have learned in this chapter, and then see if the next chapter changes or adds to your perspective.

Alma 42

Verses 27-30 complete the teachings in the last chapter. How do you feel about the Atonement, mercy, and repentance?

Alma 43

Our priorities affect the choices we make. List the priorities of the Lamanites, found in verses 8 and 29. Now list the priorities of the Nephites found in verses 9, 30, and 45. How do the differences in their priorities affect their choices and the outcome of the battle?

Alma 44

What lesson can you learn from this chapter?

Alma 45

What starts to cause problems within the Church?

Alma 46

Compare the people of Amalickiah with the people of Moroni. What are some differences?

Alma 47

How does Amalickiah become king and gain the hearts of the people?

_____

_____

_____

_____

_____

_____

_____

_____

_____

_____

_____

Alma 48

While Amalickiah manipulates and gains power over the people, what is Moroni doing? How is Moroni described here?

Alma 49

The Lamanites are surprised at the preparations made by the Nephites. What preparations do they make? What preparations do you make each day to prepare yourself for the battles you may face?

Alma 50

Even though they are at war and striving to protect their families, it says that this is the happiest time for the Nephites. Why do you think that is? How can you strive to be happy even during trying times?

_____

_____

_____

_____

_____

_____

_____

_____

_____

_____

_____

Alma 51

Amalickiah's armies conquer many of the Nephites' strongholds because of the wars and contentions among Moroni's own people (verse 22). How does contention weaken your family? What can you do to help strengthen your family?

Alma 52

In verse 19, the Nephites discuss how to "flatter" the Lamanites to leave their strongholds. How does Satan use flattery and justification to get you to leave your "strongholds"?

Alma 53

In verse 8, it says some intrigue among the Nephites cause dissensions that allow the Lamanites to take many cities. What sorts of problems between the LDS youth of your ward or school weaken you as a group? What can you do to help unify the youth in your ward or school?

Alma 54

What goes wrong in the negotiations to exchange prisoners? What could Moroni have done differently?

Alma 55

In verse 28, it says that they reclaim their rights and privileges. What are your rights and privileges as a child of God and through the covenants you have made?

Alma 56

The stripling warriors gained their strong testimonies from the teachings of their mothers. What things have your parents taught you that have helped you in life? What important things do you want to teach your children?

Alma 51

Verse 21 describes how the stripling warriors obey. How obedient are you? What does it mean to obey "every word of command with exactness"?

Alma 58

Have you ever felt like no one around you was giving you the support you need? What do Helaman and his people do during this difficult time?

Alma 59

Moroni and his chief captains begin to doubt. What do you do when you start to doubt?

Alma 60

What do you think it means in verse 23 that "the inward vessel shall be cleansed first, and then shall the outer vessel be cleansed also"?

Alma 61

Moroni makes some assumptions about Pahoran that are not true because he can only see his own afflictions and problems. Pahoran has his own problems that affect how he deals with the wars. Write about a time you assumed something about someone else or a situation. Does having more information or putting yourself in another person's shoes help you understand more clearly why someone behaves a certain way or how a situation comes to be?

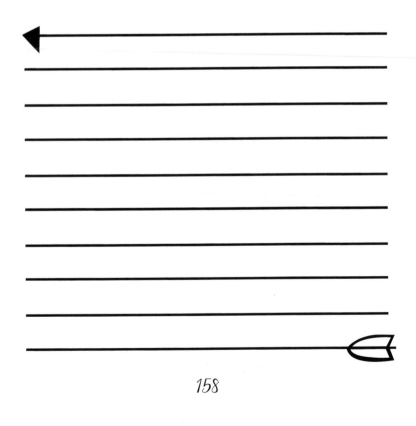

Alma 62

When you read verses 48-51, which of these things do you think helps you the most in staying strong?

Alma 63

They make copies of the scriptures to be dispersed among the people. What do you think it was like before they had copies of the scriptures?

Helaman 1

Verse 11 explains how they make a covenant, not with God but with each other, to cover up the murder of the chief judge. Why is it so damaging to make promises to someone to help them avoid the consequences of a poor choice or sin?

Helaman 2

Here we see how secret combinations become stronger. What started as a small group of people protecting one secret has now turned into a complex network of powerful people murdering and stealing. One courageous person at the beginning of this group could have stopped it. How do you gather courage to be honest and stand up for what's right?

Helaman 3

What do you think verses 29-30 mean?

_____

_____

_____

_____

_____

_____

_____

_____

_____

_____

_____

_____

Helaman 4

The slaughter of the Nephites is because of people within the Church. Verses 11-13 list the many problems happening within the Church. Which ones stand out most to you? Why?

Helaman 5

How does it describe the voice in verse 30? Have you ever heard or felt a voice like that? The Holy Ghost communicates differently to everyone. Think of an experience where you felt the Spirit. How do you hear or feel the Holy Ghost?

Helaman 6

In verse 17, it mentions that because they have been so blessed, their priorities start changing, and they start loving wealth and power. Why is it hard to keep your priorities focused on godly things when you are blessed with many material things?

Helaman 7

Nephi tells the people, "Ye have set your hearts upon the riches and the vain things of this world" (verse 21). What are the vain things of your world? How can you work to keep those things low on your priority list?

Helaman 8

Read the story of Moses and the brass serpent in Numbers 21:4-9. Nephi compares the brass serpent to Christ. Cross-reference it to Alma 33:19-20. What do you think that symbolism means, and what does it mean for you?

Helaman 9

Sometimes, when we have done wrong and we are accused, we become angry, like the judges do. What is a better reaction? Why is it hard to take responsibility for our actions? What can you do to strive to be more honest and responsible for all of your choices, including mistakes and poor choices?

Helaman 10

Why is the Lord pleased with Nephi? What is he blessed with?

Helaman 11

What are your thoughts as you read this chapter? Do you observe any patterns in the behaviors of the people?

Helaman 12

What do you think of this chapter? Do you think you are "quick to" forget the Lord and trust in Him? What does it mean to trust in the Lord?

Helaman 13

Samuel said that the city has been saved so far because of the righteous who reside there. How does your righteousness save and protect those around you?

Helaman 14

What are the signs Samuel says will accompany the birth of Christ? The death of Christ?

Helaman 15

How do you become "firm and steadfast in the faith" (verse 8)?

Helaman 16

In what ways do you depend on your own strength and your own wisdom? How can you work to rely more on the Lord's strength and wisdom?

3 Nephi 1

Even when the signs that had been prophesied come to pass, Satan works to convince people not to believe them. What are some tactics used today to justify truths and miracles and not attribute them to God?

3 Nephi 2

Four years after the signs convince most of the people to repent, they start to forget and justify and return to their wicked ways. Have there been times in your life where you quickly forget the impact of a spiritual experience? What are some things you can do to help remember those experiences and allow them to help you change for the better?

3 Nephi 3

The people gain strength by uniting together in one place and uniting their prayers and defenses. How does unifying with others who have your same goals help you? Some people are alone and need to be brought into your safe haven. Can you think of anyone you can reach out to? As you go through your week, seek for those you can bring in for strength and safety.

3 Nephi 4

The Nephites are saved, in part, because of the preparations they made and the provisions they stored. What does your family do to help prepare physically for hard times?

3 Nephi 5

What is a disciple of Christ? Are you a disciple?

3 Nephi 6

The people begin to be distinguished by ranks. Are there social "ranks" or groups that are distinguished between now? How does being divided into social groups impede God's work? What can you do help blur the social divisions you see?

3 Nephi 7

Nephi again witnesses the people forgetting the Lord and turning to wickedness. He patiently starts to preach again and gains a few converts. He does not give up on the people. Why not?

3 Nephi 8

These are the same people who saw the signs of Christ's birth thirty-three years earlier. How do you think they feel at the beginning of this chapter as they start realizing the time is soon coming when the signs of His death will come to pass?

3 Nephi 9

What does it mean to have a broken heart and contrite spirit? What does the Lord mean when He says we should be as a little child?

3 Nephi 10

What do you think of the comparison of Christ gathering us like a hen gathers her chicks under her wings? What do you think that means for the Nephites? What does it mean for you?

3 Nephi 11

How do you feel as you read this chapter? What will it be like to meet your Savior?

3 Nephi 12

In verses 3-10, Christ lists attributes we should have. Choose one and write about how you are trying to develop that attribute.

3 Nephi 13

Have you ever done service for someone secretly, without anyone knowing and without taking credit? If so, write about that experience. Make a plan to do an act of service secretly.

3 Nephi 14

What do you learn about judging from verses 1-5?

_____

_____

_____

_____

_____

_____

_____

_____

_____

_____

_____

_____

3 Nephi 15

When Christ says He has many sheep and He will unite them all into one fold, how does that apply to you?

3 Nephi 16

In verse 18, Christ says that His people will "see eye to eye." What does that mean? Does that mean they will agree on everything, or just be united? When you disagree with someone, how can you foster unification? How does seeing people the way God sees them help us with this?

3 Nephi 11

How do verses 2-3 help you devise a plan for learning the gospel? Do you ever "prepare your [mind]" before you go to church, seminary, or another spiritual activity? Afterward, do you ponder the things the Spirit has taught you? Set a goal to be more prepared in your gospel learning.

3 Nephi 18

In verse 16, Christ says that He is the Light and the Example. In verse 24, He says that we should hold up our light. What does He mean by that? How do you shine your light unto the world?

3 Nephi 19

In verse 9, it says that the thing they most desire
is to have the Holy Ghost. Do you feel like the Holy
Ghost is a precious gift? How do you feel about the
Holy Ghost and His role in your life?

3 Nephi 20

What do you think about verses 36-41?

3 Nephi 21

What do you think is the "great and . . . marvelous work" spoken of in verse 9? Do you feel like it is great and marvelous?

3 Nephi 22

In this chapter, Christ is talking to the house of Israel, but He is also talking to us. In verse 2, He asks us to enlarge our tent. One interpretation of this is that we need to be more accepting and spread the gospel to everyone. We need to enlarge our circles and our influence of who we bring to the gospel. Do you see this happening around you? What is one way you can be more accepting and bring more of your brothers and sisters to the knowledge of the gospel?

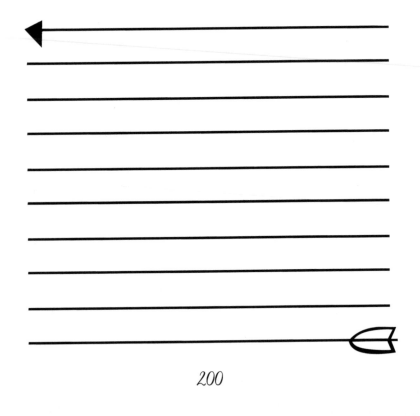

3 Nephi 23

Christ reads the scriptures they have written and mentions that some things are missing, and they add them to the record. What specific things were missing, and why do you think it was important enough that Christ asked them to add it?

3 Nephi 24

Verses 8-12 were originally written in Malachi, in the Old Testament. Christ wants them to also be written in their scriptures. How do you feel about tithing? What does Heavenly Father bless you with when you pay your tithing?

3 Nephi 25

What do you think it means to "turn the heart of the fathers to the children, and the heart of the children to their fathers" (verse 6)? Sometimes this verse is used to reference family history work. Have you done any family history work? Set a goal to find a name to take to the temple or to do some indexing.

3 Nephi 26

Verses 9 and 10 describe how we learn truths. First, we start with the small things. As we have faith and believe those things, we are given more knowledge. What "small" or basic things do you believe, and what things do you still need to work on to gain understanding and grow in your faith?

3 Nephi 21

What do you think it means to "endureth to the end" (verse 16)? Does it mean to be perfect until you die? The answer is in verse 19. Write what the answer is and how you think you personally can endure to the end.

3 Nephi 28

What do you think you would have asked for if you were one of Christ's disciples?

3 Nephi 29

What thoughts do you have as you read this chapter?

3 Nephi 30

Verse 2 lists everything we should turn away from in order to repent. Which of the things on this list do you think are among the worst problems we see in our society?

4 Nephi

What are some of the attributes the Nephites have as a group and what things are going on at the beginning of this chapter, when they are described as among the happiest of people ever to be created?

Mormon 1

What do you think it would have been like to have been Mormon?

Mormon 2

What is the difference between the sorrow the people are feeling and godly sorrow, which leads someone to repentance? Look at verses 12-14.

Mormon 3

Mormon leads the people even though they are wicked because he loves them. Is it hard when people we love are making poor choices? What are some ways God wants us to act toward those who make our lives difficult or let us down repeatedly?

Mormon 4

In verse 4, we learn that the Nephites, instead of trying to continue life in Teancum where they are protected, come up against the Lamanites. Have you ever had an experience where you made a choice you knew would have negative consequences, but you did it anyway? In verse 11, it says that their hearts are hardened, and so they continually seek after conflict and sin. How can you protect yourself and keep your heart soft?

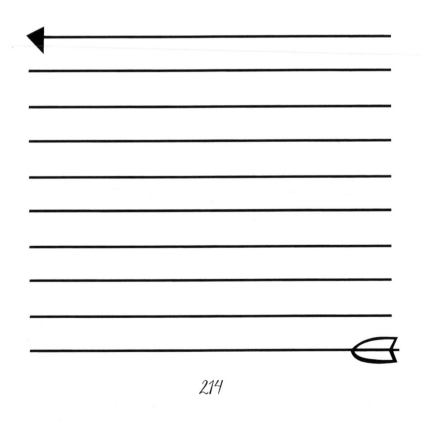

Mormon 5

In verse 2, Mormon says they "did struggle for their lives" because they do not call upon God. Do you struggle with life? How has calling upon God helped you with your struggles so far in your life?

Mormon 6

How do you feel as you read verses 16-22?

Mormon 7

These words are specifically written for the descendants of the Lamanites. Read them as if they were written for you, and write down your thoughts.

Mormon 8

Starting in verse 26, Mormon is speaking of our day. What are some thoughts you have as you read this description?

Mormon 9

What do you think when you read verse 21?

(blank writing lines)

Ether 1

The book of Ether is from the record found by the people of Limhi. The record tells of a group of people who lived during the time of the Tower of Babel and came to the American continent. What do you learn from the story of Jared asking his brother to make requests of the Lord?

Ether 2

What similarities do you find between this story and the story of Lehi and his family at the beginning of the Book of Mormon? As you read the first six chapters of Ether, read the story as an allegory of your journey through life and write down any insights that come to you.

Ether 3

What are your thoughts as you read the story of the Lord showing Himself to the brother of Jared?

Ether 4

Verse 12 says that anything that "persuadeth men to do good" comes from Christ. Does that mean only members of the Church can do the Lord's work?

Ether 5

Who are the witnesses spoken of in this chapter? Why do you think the Lord uses multiple witnesses in doing His work?

Ether 6

Remember that this story is also a parable about your journey in life. What verses in this chapter have symbolism that relates to your journey? Notice verses 6 and 7. How can you make your "barge" tight so you will be safe from the crashing waves and deepness of the ocean?

Ether 7

The desire for power causes a lot of contention. Notice the patterns of family members trying to usurp the kingdom from each other. Family relationships are among the most difficult and rewarding relationships we can have during our lives. Are there ever power struggles in your family? What can you do to stay humble and avoid power struggles?

Ether 8

Here we see the establishment of secret combinations among the Jaredites. What do you see in our society today that could be equated to secret combinations?

Ether 9

This chapter seems like a summary of the Book of Mormon: righteousness, prosperity, pride, trials, humility, mercy, repentance, righteousness. Do you see this cycle in your life? What can you do to break the cycle?

Ether 10

Under the leadership of Lib, the people become prosperous again. Each time the people become prosperous, it mentions how hard they work. In this instance, they are described as "industrious" (verse 22). What role does hard work have in our prosperity? Do you have a personal experience with how hard work helps you?

Ether 11

Verse 8 shows us that regardless of how many times we make mistakes, the Lord will always have mercy on us when we repent. Write your feelings on this.

Ether 12

In verse 27, we learn that weaknesses are an important part of life. Why are weaknesses important? What are some of your weaknesses, and how can they be made into your strengths?

Ether 13

Why does Ether have to hide in a cave? Imagine you were Ether; what would that be like?

_____

_____

_____

_____

_____

_____

_____

_____

_____

_____

_____

Ether 14

There is symbolism in verses 1-2. All of their things kept disappearing. It causes them to "cleave unto that which was his own," and they "would not borrow neither would he lend" (verse 2). When we become materialistic, we start to value our things over the things of God, and we start becoming selfish. Do you have things you "cleave" to? What can you do to make sure you cleave to your covenants and your relationship with Heavenly Father and Christ over the material things you have in this life?

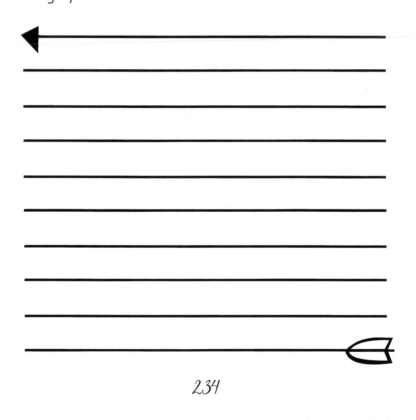

Ether 15

Compare the description of the people in verse 19 to the description of the people during the time of Mormon. Even though Coriantumr starts repenting, the Spirit is gone and their hearts are hardened. In verse 3, it says that Coriantumr is so sorrowful, he refuses to be comforted. Sometimes when we repent, we want to suffer and beat ourselves up and we don't accept the comfort from the Savior. Have you had an experience like this? What does the Savior want for you when you have made a mistake? What words would He say to you if you felt deep sorrow for your mistakes like Coriantumr did?

Moroni 1

Moroni has no home. He has to wander and hide because the people hate him for his beliefs. Have you ever felt prejudice because of your beliefs or standards? What did you do about it? If not, what would you do in that situation?

Moroni 2

The next few chapters are things Moroni wants to tell the Lamanites. They have to do with how to organize the Church. What is the first thing he wants them to know?

Moroni 3

Why is it important that God's authority is given in this way?

Moroni 4

Read this prayer and think about it. What are you promising each Sunday when you take the bread, and what promises does Heavenly Father give you?

Moroni 5

How is this prayer different from the prayer on the bread?

Moroni 6

What do you learn from this chapter?

Moroni 7

How are faith, hope, humility, and charity connected? Charity is said to be the greatest, and it is the pure love of Christ. What does that mean to you? How do you think you can develop charity?

Moroni 8

What are the blessings of repentance listed in verse 26?

Moroni 9

How do verses 3-6 relate to you?

Moroni 10

Moroni gives us a challenge to pray to know if the Book of Mormon is true. Will you take his challenge? Write down the experience you have had while reading this book and your experience after praying to know if it is true.